The Other Side of Orphan

By

Terry Barlow

3/12/2021

The Other Side of Orphan

Terry Barlow

VANTAGE PRESS
New York

Cover illustration by Jamie Barlow

FIRST EDITION

Published by Vantage Press, Inc.
516 West 34th Street, New York, New York 10001

Manufactured in the United States of America
ISBN: 0-533-14082-X

Library of Congress Catalog Card No.: 01-126948

0 9 8 7 6 5 4 3 2 1

To my devoted wife, Leslyn, who paid a high price in sweat and tears to make this possible

God knows forever . . . and we all know so much that we didn't know that we knew . . . and feel so much that we didn't know that we felt.

Contents

Addendum

Foreword

Its OK to be . . .

Some years ago, and I've known Terry Barlow for some years, he said to another, "It's OK to be you." At that point in time, it was a word that needed to be heard, a word in due season, a word that sets one free.

The Other Side of Orphan is a collection of such words. Fit words in due season. Words that challenge your view of how things are or of how they should be.

Terry has a way of taking the ordinary things of life and looking at them with a fresh lens. A lens that can set one free of crooked thoughts that twist our ideas and hold us back from the freedom of our creation.

In this day of non-stop motion Terry validates the need to "sit and be." Where " . . . nothing is more important than just being, and seeing where being leads." With a play on words, a shift in letters, a juxtapositioning of ideas, he arrests your thoughts to bring fresh insight.

Yet while the world is moving faster each day, there are an increasing number of us wishing to find that quiet place within the center of our being. As we tackle that formidable task Terry gives us encouragement with "The Bread:"

> Jesus, taking the bread, broke it and said, "This is my body, broken for you. This is my body, I never said it was a piece of cake."

I hope that you find *The Other Side of Orphan* a thoughtful and uplifting respite from a frequently too busy world.

—Dr. Glenn Mehltretter, Ed.D.
President, PeopleFit℠
Organizational Design Consultants
Raleigh, North Carolina
12/20/01

Preface

There is a word for one who has no functioning parents: orphan. There is a word for one who loses a husband: widow. And there is a word for one who loses a wife: widower. But there is no word for a parent who loses a child. Like a father who loses his only son. There is no word for such a one. That could be because that particular hurt is unspeakable.

Author's Note

Whatever our philosophies, whatever our goals, whatever our respective visions may be, they will be the healthier for resting squarely on this truth among others, this truth among truths: WE ALL MAKE MISTAKES OFTEN. If we see ourselves and all others in that merciful light, we will be much the better for it!

Introduction

We all know so much that we don't know that we know, much of it on an intuitive level. This book is a journey through the mediums of meditation, Scripture, dialogue, poetry, proverb, and humor into the inner regions of Christ where the wealth of our knowing is located. These writings are intended as seeds that will blossom in our changed relationships with ourselves and others.

Too long we have looked outward to everyone and everything but our own redeemed selves for enlightenment. *The Other Side of Orphan* facilitates a change in that tendency and helps us to an increasing acceptance of ourselves, our losses, and our own peculiar processes of transformation.

The Other Side of Orphan

Part I:

Father

A Wild Idea

I have this wild idea that eyes flowing
with tears are made
more beautiful thereby,
And cheeks streaming down
softer complexion create,
And the choke in the throat
clears the way for
truer words to speak,
And the throb in the breast
the inner person keeping
beat to a rare and distant song.

Recipe for Frustration

Why does he seem so frustrated?
Because he has this particular goal.
That in itself shouldn't frustrate him, unless it is an unreasonable goal.
His goal is to pass through this life without experiencing a single trial or difficulty . . . and he is fiercely determined.
God help him.
God can't help him.

When Are We Right?

Once when I was in college at Rutgers, one of my housemates asked a rather obscure (at least for that time) question about the Bible, something to do with the Book of Ruth, I think.

I knew the answer. I blurted it out immediately. It was a strange feeling I had. I knew but I had no idea *how* I knew. I had stored that incident away in a place that, until then, had collected not so much. I remember my housemates being very impressed, and I remember acting so nonchalant as though, of course they should expect me to know. As I look back on that incident now, I see in it the first rudiments of the call of God being heard and received into my life.

On another occasion I told a girlfriend, "I feel a greatness inside of me." And then I asked, and this may have been my downfall, "Does that sound arrogant to you?"

What she answered in effect but not in so many words was, "YES."

Both of us couldn't have been right, or could we have been? For God Who Is Always Right and Who wants so badly for us to be, gave His Son to be wrong for us . . . and the arrogance is draining away.

Deficit-minded

I must make it up!
That is the space I've been crowded out of by the builders.
I must make it up!
That is the time all the time I've lost waiting at these stoplights.
I must make it up.
That is the money that was due but denied me.
I must make it up!
That is all the fun I could have had if I hadn't chosen to be bored.
I must make it up!
That is the life I won't ever be living.

Advice

I once received wise advice from a dying woman, advice that I have considered many times since: "Drive your convertible with the top down and your hat off, don't worry about your hair."

She seemed to be talking about more than convertibles.

Beyond Fun

There's nothing wrong with having fun sometimes.
There's nothing wrong with having fun *most* of the time.
Why not *all* the time then?
Well, maybe fun wouldn't be fun if it was all the time.
And if fun was supposed to be most of the time but turned out not to be, would we think there was something wrong with us that we weren't having so much fun?
And thinking that way might we forfeit that little fun of which we *were* capable?
Reaching for so much only to lose then even the little.
We can permit ourselves to be ordinary, allow ourselves our own ordinariness.
The religious calendar has time between the holy seasons called "ordinary time."
A time to reflect on what has already happened.
Or a time to prepare for what or who is coming.

The Mammoth

There was this mammoth personal problem,
a feeling frozen long ago,
like a great mammoth in its block of ice,
grass still protruding
from its teeth,
green as it was, oh so long ago.
There is this mammoth personal problem
whose ice is melting tears,
the water dripping down its huge flanks,
the grass sliding from its teeth,
down down to earth
again.

Heaven

I woke from a half-sleep, lamenting the fact that we all lead such separate lives but talk, on the other hand, of being one. It's not that there's anything we can do about it. It's part and parcel of who we are by definition. We experience most of our moments alone. We live through ourselves.

Heaven is that rarefied state in which we live through one another. There is an essential sadness about anything less than that.

Sorry Face

I have a happy face
    I want the world to see
And I have a sorry face
    that I keep alone for me.
I lift it to the stars
    and I lift it to the sun,
Wherever I am sure
    that I'm the only one.
I have a sorry face
    that no one else must see.
The world's weight of sorrow
    doth twist it like a tree.

A Perfect Day

Some days are so good that I don't want them to ever end. Even the clothes that I am wearing seem so right I don't want to take them off. So I lay those clothes to rest, rather mournfully, and, as I climb into bed, I lament the fact that such a wonderful day ever has to pass, a day in which I carried myself so lightly so as to simply glide over the path.

The Great Theft of Essences

The Land of Almost.

That was the place where nothing seemed quite itself and no one was quite whom they appeared to be. And it was not really the time of day that it seemed to be or the exact place one would have thought. Neither was it that juncture in history that it was cracked up to be when I first recognized the place. But unless one knew better, one wouldn't know the difference.

That was the key to it. No one really knew oneself or anyone else or anything else well enough to recognize the poor imitations all around. This fundamental ignorance perpetuated the illusion of it all. And so it went.

People would say, "I'm not really myself today" or "You seem different," without knowing the full significance of what they had said. So nobody truly knew what he or she was talking about, but it didn't seem to matter because nobody quite knew the difference.

The Lofty Realm of the Really Important

I've often wondered what the really important people do all day. They must do really important things. Their days must be measured very carefully so as not to waste a moment. Their skills and intelligence have to be exploited to the maximum. I just don't imagine them spinning their wheels as I sometimes do, or staring blankly out a window, or straightening a tabletop three different ways when the first way didn't matter to begin with. They would probably never dash downstairs to place a meaningless scrap of paper in a wastebasket that was more nearly empty than the one upstairs. I just don't feature them wondering things like whether 1923 seemed as modern in 1923 as 2001 seems in 2001 to their grandchildren.

What? See what—I told you so. There just isn't time for that sort of nonsense. Like whether the new Volkswagen Beetle would have looked weird to Rudolph Valentino. Who cares! There's no time for that kind of ruminating, among the really important, I mean. It's just not productive; that's it, no way.

A Word Expressed

The Greek word *agapas* existed before the time of Christ, but was rarely used. It was the life and ministry of Jesus Christ that called the reality of the meaning of that word into play in human history. It is a word that means an unselfish kind of love that is able to give without expecting anything in return. Jesus made that a reality in everyday life.

Similarly, each of us is meant to bring out of dormancy a new shade of meaning of the reality of the truth of God. Perhaps it is not a new meaning or a new word because it has always been in the mind of God, but it never had the chance to be *embodied* as it has now that you have been birthed into the family of God.

Acquainted

I like the traditional choice of words in the fifty-third chapter of the Book of Isaiah where it reads that Jesus was *acquainted* with grief as a man of sorrows. Jesus was an acquaintance of grief but not a *friend* of grief. He did not warm up and cozy up to grief so as to become too comfortable with it. He would not let himself be consumed by it, but neither would he ignore it as though it didn't exist.

Jesus allowed himself to be touched by grief, but not to be dragged away by it. He was acquainted with grief.

Letting Go

God does not call us to give things up so much as to let things go. One can give something up without letting it go, and one can let something go without necessarily giving it up.

Paradox

If faith is calling those things that be not as though they were, then denial is sometimes calling that which *is* as though it were not.

What Is to Come

When some provision or blessing to which we are accustomed ceases to flow into our lives, it is very often so that something else of beauty can appear, something that has been within us sleeping all the time. Consider the autumn leaves; the pigments of yellow and gold, and blazing orange, only appear when the chlorophyl supply is squeezed shut.

Think of this in your deprivation, when you behold the pageant of autumn, another quality that God cherishes is beginning to beautifully manifest in your life.

Prayer Journey

When on the journey of prayer, we reach the nations bordering our own; it is normal to converse with other tongues, foreign tongues. Jesus did say, come to think of it, that His Temple was to be a house of prayer for the nations.

Listen

We are no better at hearing the voice of God than we are at listening to the most personal messages from our own bodies.

In Spite Of

I heard Hope admit,
    "I'm in despair,"
but didn't see a quitter
    anywhere.
I heard Courage stammer,
    "I'm afraid,"
and then mount her stallion
    for the raid.

I heard Joy confide,
    "I feel so sad,"
but it saved her mind
    from going mad.

Health

Hugraino is the Greek word from which we get the English word "hygiene." It not only means to be free from sickness, it also means to be void of germs that produce sickness. As in the case of AIDS, one may not have the disease itself, but one can be infected with the HIV virus that produces AIDS as a matter of course.

It is dubious consolation for someone infected with the HIV virus to know that he or she has not technically contracted AIDS yet.

Saved

The Bible tells us to be transformed by the renewal of our minds, not *conformed* by the *removal* of our minds.

We are not saved from having to think.

Being

There are times when a person wants to do nothing other than sit and *be*. If at all possible, that person does well to do precisely that and no more: sit and be, hold a sitting bee. What is so curious is that when one would expect to feel restless from just sitting, one feels a sense of rest instead. At other times the restlessness that arises is a prompting to get moving because there are important things to do. But during a sitting bee, or better yet, a be-in, nothing is more important than just being, and seeing where being leads.

One doesn't dodge a needful be-in because of important priorities. But rather one dodges a needful be-in because of *impotent* priorities.

Lite

How terrible that we should have to refer to ourselves as wretches when singing a hymn to Him. This is certainly beneath our dignity as upstanding Christians! And why should we have to read about ourselves as "mere worms" when faithfully reading our weekly portion of Old Testament?

Furthermore why do we always have to be subjected to such gore even in our dutiful reading of the New Testament? Must we hear incessantly about the blood, the blood, the blood? We recommend hereby the publication of new Lite Hymnals, and an Old Testament Lite and a New Testament Lite, more in keeping with the spirit of the times! Yes, the new Cliff Notes Bible!

True Love

Some of us occupy ourselves or preoccupy ourselves with others because we despise ourselves. Until our love for others flow out of a healthy appreciation for ourselves, it will never be the true love that extends to preferring one another.

One doesn't prefer another in the biblical sense out of disgust for oneself. That must first be worked through; otherwise there's no contest.

Advise and consent does not spring from despise and resent.

Listen Up!

If I respect myself, I will listen to the signals my body is sending me and respond accordingly. If it's saying, "I've had enough to eat," then I will stop eating. If it's saying, "I'm hungry," then I will pause to eat. If it's saying, "I'm tired," then I will rest, and if it's saying, "I have no sexual desire or very little desire," then I will not force the issue.

I do this out of respect for my body, which translates into respect for myself. To ignore these basic messages would indicate a disrespect, even a dislike for myself, just as it would if I blatantly ignored another person who was attempting to address me. The very least I can do is to hear the person out.

Uneroded

We read some chapters from John's gospel. They were the same as when I had read them twenty years before. And they were the same as when they had been read by so many others for hundreds of years before that. I thought of all the daily newspapers over that time—how they change from day to day, and of all the books and magazines, and broadcasts—how they come and how they go, along with films and videos quickly forgotten.

But the Word of God remains forever; that is a comfort to know.

Prying

I had the distinct impression that I was being analyzed, yet I had not come to a psychiatrist or a therapist nor had I asked for therapy or psychiatric treatment. But it seemed that statements were being made and questions were being asked to test me through the nature of my response. I asked myself if I was merely imagining things, but even so, since I didn't usually feel this way, there was something about this kind of person that helped to stimulate such imaginings.

The bottom line was that I could not fully relax because I was continually wondering what she might be trying to uncover as she asked herself, so I imagined, "Now what does he *really* mean by that?" While all along what I meant, as far as I knew, was simply what I had said.

Gravity

The most urgent matters of prayer are not the ones that first occur to us. Like a container of water in which the heaviest particles settle first toward the bottom while the lighter particles hover nearer the surface where they are more likely to gain immediate attention, so is the patient practice of prayer.

Like an upright container of water, sediment and all, what is uppermost in our minds matters least. Upon what is buried, everything depends.

Part II:

Son

Time Warp

What time is it?
Two o'clock.
This clock says three.
What are you doing?
I'm resetting it.
But you're going the long way; you only have to go back one.
No, you have to go *with* the numbers.
Are you trying to be clock wise?
Are you trying to counter clockwise?
I guess that makes me clock foolish.
Yeah, dwelling on the past.

Homeless

There are increasing numbers of homeless individuals and homeless families who are wandering throughout our nation. Although some choose that lifestyle, there are many in the streets through no choice of their own. Similarly, there has been an epidemic of homelessness developing on the spiritual level, again often involving entire families that are the victims of church splits or runaway and delinquent pastors. In other cases persons who consider themselves believers are simply more comfortable not making the commitment needed to identify with a local church. The consequent weakening of the church in general due to increasing numbers of those without church homes is not unrelated, as a cause, to the worsening surface social problem of displaced people and homelessness.

If asked why they left churches or why they have never committed to any, many of these spiritually homeless will say, "The church was dead" or "They didn't preach the Bible." This is a case of one extreme position pointing for justification to the other extreme position while ignoring the width of spectrum in-between of living, biblically-based churches that desperately need the gifts of their errant critics and the support they could provide.

The Dream

The network news team was conducting a survey. Up and down the street, they went asking, "What do you think of topless dancing establishments?"

> "We don't want them around here, we've got children."
> "Well, as long as they keep it clean and under control
> and don't expose the younger people."
> "I don't see anything wrong with it."

Then they singled out a man in a white tee-shirt: "Hey, it's great, I like it," he said without hesitating.

On his tee-shirt was a picture of Martin Luther King with the famous exclamation: "I have a dream."

Reverend King had a dream all right, but I'm not sure it was what the man in the tee-shirt had in mind.

Fidelity

Convenient fidelity is being faithful only as long as there is no opportunity to be otherwise. Covenant fidelity is being faithful no matter what and no matter who. (Notice how covenant words like "fidelity," "trust," "mutual," and "union" have been co-opted by banking institutions.)

I attended primary school in a big building that housed all grades up through high school. Often when I would enter the building in the morning, I would encounter a high school couple arguing. It was always the same couple, and the girl was always crying. This constant reminder, combined with my parents example, gave me the early impression that relationships between the opposite sexes were fraught with unhappiness, with bickering, petty jealousies and resentments. Today I an gradually unlearning that fateful conclusion. I say with W. B. Yeats to that little boy at the side entrance to school, to that little boy who I was,

> For the world is more full of weeping
> Than you can understand.

But it doesn't have to be that way. There is a promise of a better way. Come—and take a look.

Now I see a couple holding hands, looking rapturously into each other's eyes; they turn standing shoulder to shoulder and a radiance emits from them and begins to envelop me as they smile and motion to me to come. . . .

No wait a minute. This is from one extreme to the other. The Truth is somewhere in between.

Experience

Early in the believer's experience, we may reject certain values that we once cherished only to embrace them again later in life when they can be better integrated. It is not that those jettisoned values were wrong in themselves, but in comparison with the One we have newly encountered, they are, or cannot help but be rejected for that time being.

If we truly understood the suffering of another, most of what we say to that one would be left unsaid. We have to pass through the same kind of suffering ourselves to even be eligible for that understanding.

Cold Light

A firefly produces light by the oxidation of luciferin, a pigment located in spots on the sides of its abdomen and thorax. The interesting thing about the light is that it is not only intermittent but *heatless.*

The pigment luciferin takes its name from Lucifer, meaning light-bearer. Lucifer's light is heatless in the sense that it is loveless. His wisdom isn't tempered with love; in fact, it is merciless and cruel in its consequences.

Two and One

With my two ears, I will listen at least twice as much as I speak with my one mouth. I will hear people out, make sure I get it the way they mean it, and then I will have my say, based in part, at least, on what I have just heard. That's communication. Sounds simple enough . . . doesn't it?

Inside Out

You say that from the moment we are born we are busy dying.

I say that until the day we die, we are busy being born!

Therein lies the fundamental difference between us.

Turning the Tables

The day that Stephen died, he preached to the crowd in such a way that it cut to the quick of their hearts. The word of God, the sword of the Spirit, was performing a slicing circumcision of the heart upon the people as Stephen spoke. It was not well received by the people; they became angry and resistant to the work that God wanted to do in their hearts that very moment. They did not think that, as they turned hatefully upon the instrument of what might have been their deliverance, they were turning against God Himself.

They couldn't get over their resentment of the fact that Stephen had turned the tables on them, as Jesus had turned the tables on the money-changers.

Per Se

A male is not per se a man.
A mate is not per se a husband or a wife.
A female is not per se a woman.
To sire is not per se to parent.

Parents were those who held us snugly against the ugly.

The Slip

Then they took up stones to cast at him; but Jesus hid himself, and went out of the temple, going through the midst of them, and so passed by.

Therefore they sought again to take him: but he escaped out of their hand.

. . . And rose up and cast him out of the city, and led him to the brow of the hill on which their city was built, that they might cast him down headlong. But he, passing through the midst of them, went his way. (John 8:59, 10:39, Luke 8:59)

Jesus had a nimble, unrehearsed way of slipping out of tight spots, the same as he had a way of talking himself out of corners and through loaded questions. I don't even suppose he knew exactly how he did it; it seemed to come so naturally. There was a "slipperiness" about him because of the thick anointing on his life, until the time that he obediently offered up even that, allowing himself to be caught. But the way he got out of that final bind was the slipperiest of all the slips!

Handicaps

There are many handicaps in this life. For example, there is the lack of sight, or the lack of hearing, or the lack of mobility, but it occurs to me that the greatest handicap of all may be (worse than the lack of education) what is commonly perceived as the lack of time.

Somewhere in the sea is the rock she skipped forty years ago with her friends on the beach when there was something to say and someone to listen, someone who had time. Somewhere in the sea that rock sits so quietly now—as she does, leaning heavily to one side.

Blessings

It can be a blessing to be hated to the point of even being persecuted; it can make the time spent, however brief, with those who love us, however few, that much sweeter.

An Anchor

Today I was lying on my back by the edge of the pool and my wife, Leslyn, was floating on a raft in the water beside me. We were holding hands. I let go of her hand for a moment to arrange myself more comfortably when she said, "Honey, don't let go. If you don't hold my hand, I'll *drift.*" She chuckled. "You're my anchor."

I knew the deeper truth of her simple statement. When I show my wife affection in such simple gestures, I am acting as a reliable anchor for her and for our relationship.

Husbands, love your wives as Christ loved the Church and gave himself for her. (Ephesians 5, verse 25)

The Spreading Spirit

Just as when the body dies, the spirit of that body is released, so when a person dies to self (selfishness or self-centeredness), there follows a release of that one's spirit while still alive in the body. The spirit expands and flows forth in a much richer measure to perform and fulfill the purpose for which it was created. One is actually more present to one's true self than one ever was before this time of dying to selfish desire and ambition, and pride. There is no limit to how selfish people can become when they really commit themselves to it.

We know that Jesus was more present in spirit than he ever was in the flesh. He became more present *after* his death because then His spirit was given. In spirit, He was more present in His absence than He ever was in His physical presence. And so it is that we become more present when we are absent from our lusting and coveting, and competing. And if we are more present, we are more present to others. And having died and been buried (as our baptism experience reminds us), we are yet alive with His resurrection life!

Memories

I am beginning to understand why my older friend became so angry at my losing the pressed flower from betwixt the pages of her favorite poems, and then assuring her (so long ago) that it really didn't matter.

Armor

When I embrace any brother or sister (including myself), I am placing on them the armor of Christ. When I speak to any (including myself) the encouraging and enlightening word, I am handing them the sharpened sword.

Marriage

The following question came out of a dream; "Can a canonical marriage ever be in vain?"

The following answer came out of the same dream; "No, but it can be very humbling."

Marriage is not primarily about happiness; it is about commitment. Learning this, however, we become immediately happier.

Intrusion

It occurs to me that at least part of what it means for the "abomination of desolations" to intrude upon and stand within the Holy Place is seen in the merchandising of intimacy that has become so rampant lately. It is as though the ache of loneliness has become so unbearable in our society that it is spawning more and more desperate measures to try to salve it, like the confession lines and "love connections" that are filling television time increasingly with shameless advertising and false promises.

The lure of sex is being used to prey upon people in the lonely voids of their lives through a barrage of sensually provocative imagery to gain monetary profit from them. These advertisers are trivializing the human need for someone to listen and to care. And that is treading on sacred ground.

Talk

It's therapeutic to talk with a neighbor, stream of consciousness like, about what you actually think about or feel. Most of the time we don't talk about what we think about or feel; instead we just talk about what we talk about.

Wisdom

Two friends had traveled across a continent together. One night they met a wise man from the East with whom they conversed at length, trying the wings of their philosophies. The wine was flowing freely, and finally one of the friends boldly asked, "Will you tell me which of us is more intelligent, my friend or myself? You are wise. I am sure that you recognize intelligence when you see it."

The wise man immediately motioned toward the other friend who had not spoken.

The one who asked was flabbergasted. "But why?" he inquired again.

"Because the question itself is lacking in intelligence," was the reply.

Knowledge

"Here comes that good man," a lady said, as we entered the lobby.

"What do you mean? You don't even know his name!?"

"She doesn't know his name," I answered, "but she knows his heart."

“It”

When we were children, we used to play “tag” and someone was always “it.” When we became adults, we learned
an adult version of tag: I think I am “It” and I go around
tagging you with guilt or blame, or criticism.

Legitimacy

A child is not illegitimate because it doesn't know it's father; a child is illegitimate because it is undisciplined. A child may know its father quite well and yet remain undisciplined. Such a child will not respect its parents or guardian. Some of the most intimate moments between parent and child come following discipline when the parent is there for the child, and when the child allows the parent to be there and to console. A child is legitimate whose parenting person is there for the child as the child allows this to happen. All discipline begins with the the look or the word and advances to a stage of action if need be.

A Solution

An elderly woman asked me to take her for a ride in her wheelchair, but I could not budge the brake-release, so the chair and the woman sat motionless. Later I found another person struggling with the same wheelchair and asking for my help. I tried again to release the break but without success. Finally out of frustration, I began to strike at the lever with the butt of my hand; it gave way and the chair began to roll.

As I reflect on that experience, I realize that there are some problems that are not well addressed by a soft and gentle approach. In fact, there may be no graceful way to solve them. They require a certain amount of raw force.

Effort

Most married couples would agree that there are areas in which each would like to see the other partner change. It was a revelation for me to realize recently that the changes themselves are less important than the fact that the other is making an effort to please his or her mate. That is a matter of character, whereas the actual changes themselves may or may not be.

This is also true of changes we would like to see in ourselves. That we are being conscientious toward those ends is more significant in the long run than the actual results.

Impact

I learned of an interesting farming practice used in Bible times. Flocks of sheep and goats were led up and down the fields where seed had been sown to drive the seed deeper into the soil. This would result in a larger and stronger root system.

It is so in our earthly walk with the Lord and his people. The seed of His word is driven deeper into our being by the commerce and concourse of the flocks, by our interactions with the various peoples of God, and our diverse dealings with them, and theirs with us.

Making Do

JESUS took the twelve up a mountain to ordain them. The word "ordain" or "appoint" comes from a Greek word from which we derive the English words "poem" or "poet," or "poetry." The Greek word means "make" or "do." Put those together and we have "make-do." Jesus was making do with what He had. Same as He asks us to do. It wasn't that the apostles were so great, but that He would be great in them despite their seeming mediocrity.

"Hi, Bye"

My wife's brother had an ornament in his yard by the front porch. It said "Hi" on one side and "Bye" on the other side that faced people as they were leaving. We noticed that the "Bye" side was still new-looking as though freshly painted. The "Hi" side was kinda worn out and barely legible. We wondered if that was because so many had overstayed their welcome.

A Kiss

If I plant a kiss
    upon your cheek,
Then what will grow there?
What does a kiss look like
    when it blossoms? I know,
A rose, a rosy cheek.

Thick Skins

People of God! Thicken your skins, for millions are pressing into the valley of decision, and thousands are filing into the valley within that valley. Have thick skins, I tell you. They will not all decide as you hoped they would. In fact most won't. Most won't, and in most cases it is nothing personal, so please don't take it that way. You don't have to because I, The Lord, will take it personally enough for all of you.

Loving

"And having loved his own who were in this world, he loved them to the end." That is, he loved them to the end of love. Think of love as a journey that we embark on in marriage or friendship and community. It is like a long tunnel through the massive mountain of life. Many turn around and go back. Jesus went the full distance of love, through every shade of its meaning, every season of its year.

Part III:

“Spirit”

The Source

We look to Jesus to be what we are not and then try to imitate him in that, but Jesus wants to be who we are *with* us while still being himself within us. If Jesus as a young man, for example, had been left out of a game because of lack of skill, we would have expected him to register no emotion but gladness that no one else had to suffer the hurt. But we have it backwards. The reason he can feel our pain is that he first felt keenly his *own* human pain. It is a delusion, and a cruel one at that, to think we can feel others' pain without first feeling our own, and there is no true compassion for others apart from compassion for ourselves.

The big pan slammed to the floor behind the counter at Hardee's and the whole place vibrated for a few seconds. Every eye turned toward the sheepish offender. I turned toward the man beside me, and we winced in pain together. So that is what a gift is like without the love to go with it, a clanging cymbal.

Spewing

Jesus says in Revelation, the third chapter, that he wishes the Laodiceans were either hot or cold, that since they are neither hot nor cold, only lukewarm, he will spit them out of his mouth. The Greek word translated "spit" is actually the word for "vomit," which, to think about it, is usually an involuntary reaction from our bodies. This seems to imply that Jesus has no real choice in the matter other than to reject the one who is lukewarm, since that is the automatic reaction of his holy nature toward such a one.

Perspective

No matter how pleasant the set of circumstances, the longer I look at them on a purely horizontal level, the sooner I will become depressed by those very same circumstances.

No matter how dismal the circumstances, the longer I look at them through a vertical lens (that is, from the perspective of a relationship to God), the more cause I will find to rejoice.

Honest

In order to walk, we have to begin where we are and take one step at a time. It is no different in our walk with God. We begin where we are. We are honest with Him, admit our true condition, and begin from there, first things first—one thing at a time. God, for His part, will reciprocate with an honesty that we can accommodate but that may startle us nonetheless. As God is a God of peace, it is only natural that His communications to us will have a *disarming* quality about them.

Singing

A preoccupied person cannot sing (or dance, for that matter) in the true sense of the word. Neither can a worried person. Worried, preoccupied people do not even think of singing. Singing implies a certain carefree lightheartedness on the part of the singers. Singing implies a kind of freedom on the part of the singers; they are free enough to sing! When singing is reduced to a mere ritual, it has become a form that is empty of the wine of freedom that once filled it. It has ceased to be singing in the true sense of the word. It is for us to rediscover the spontaneity of the songs that singers sing because they are free.

"If you want joy, you can sing for it" is true enough, but it is equally true that if we sing, it is because we *are* joyful.

Seduction

I felt two things in sequence, very strongly. One that the pleasures of this earth were conspiring, with my cooperation, to make such a passive creature of me, when there was so much to be done, so much that God wanted to pour into and through my life, so heartbreakingly much, with my cooperation . . . my *diligent* cooperation.

Second, the initial frustration of seeing those earthly pleasures upon which my heart was most fixed dangling just out of reach of late appearing increasingly as a noticeable pattern until it began to be a matter of no consequence whether I ever reached them. It seems that those are the very areas in which my heart does not yet belong to God who in His great love and mercy toward me is trying to remedy the situation.

Time

There is a way of being with God that actually *creates time*. Though time elapses during such an exercise, one actually finds that by some mystery when it is done, one has more time for things than at the beginning of it. But the truth of the matter is that one is never really "done" with it.

Worship

The word "worship" comes from the Old English "worthship." The best therapy for a low sense of self-worth is to worship God in spirit and truth. In fact, our word "therapy" comes from the ancient Greek verb *therapeau,* which is one of the words for worship. To worship God is to become one with the Being who places inestimable value upon each of us.

Use It

There is no art that diminishes as quickly with disuse as that art of worshiping God. There is no skill that fades so rapidly without practice as the practice of praise. There is no blade that dulls so soon without attention as the blade of the sword of the Word of God.

The Bread

Jesus, taking the bread, broke it and said, "This is my body, broken for you. This is *my body.* I never said it was a piece of cake."

Amazing

God said to me, "You amaze me. You amaze me because of what you *don't* know by now. And you amaze me because of what you *do* know already!"

Healing

In our emphasis that Jesus suffered *for* us, we lose sight of the simple example that He gave in the *way* He suffered, making His sufferings a source of healings for others. We are to follow this example in our own sufferings in making them too a source of wholeness for others as well as ourselves. We cannot avoid the fact of suffering in our lives even though Jesus suffered for us. In fact Jesus told us that we would suffer since we, as servants, are not above our master. But He has not told us that without teaching us to make those same sufferings count for others, even as He did his own, right up to making His death count most of all.

Union

The union of flesh with flesh can only produce that which is dying from the start. But the union of spirit with spirit produces only that which lives forever, whether that union be ours with God or ours with one another's spirit through God. The union of flesh with flesh produces the possibility of eternal life, but the union of spirit with spirit produces the certainty of it.

A Mustard Seed

Hear ye, hear ye. A vital distinction must here be drawn between mustard-seed faith and what I choose to call muster-seed faith. Muster-seed faith is the fatal kind that we muster up ourselves from within ourselves to fulfill our concept of what a believer should do and be (in that order).

Mustard-seed faith, on the other hand, is the faith of Jesus Himself, which grows within us as a seed grows gradually and sprouts, becoming what we did not imagine in our wildest dreams it ever becoming, something that in no way resembles the seed that started it all. It is essential to remember in this that we are already doing as a matter of course those things that not long ago we deemed and declared to be frighteningly impossible!

A Mountain and a Plain

Jesus preached a Sermon on the Mount and a sermon on the plain as if to give both perspectives and tell a more complete story, knowing that a plain is best seen from a mountain and a mountain is best glimpsed from the plain. (In the same way, He took James, Peter, and John aside to see both His ecstasy on the Mount of Transfiguration and, later, His agony in Gethsemane.)

Greenhouse Effect

God has His own “greenhouse effect” that corresponds to the natural one our earth is currently experiencing; it is an intensified, idealized spiritual environment where saints can mature quickly and quietly for imminent use in His purposes.

Laughter

God will bring to pass, as He did with Sarah, those things that would provoke spontaneous laughter from us to hear of them, those things that cannot be rationally determined ahead of time. We laugh because they seem so impossibly contrary to our ability or character.

Denial

If we don't face the reality of our situation with prayer, we will evade it with denial, denial that intensifies according to the persistence of truth until the breaking point.

(In sinking beneath the waves and in later denying his Lord, Peter was an example of the *best* faith and love that the apostles indeed, the world, had to offer at that time.)

Picked

Jesus picked us; we did not pick Him. But our version of it, sometimes, is that He picked *on* us. (We add that little preposition, which is our "no" to Him spelled backwards.)

Close

I consider my thoughts to be even closer to me than my breath, and my feelings seem even closer than that. But the Holy Spirit is closer than all of these thoughts and feelings (which, though silent, are amplified in the ear of God).

Grieving

The Holy Spirit can be grieved. It occurs to me that grief is usually experienced over a death or a similar deep loss. We grieve the Holy Spirit when we become as though dead before God, when we become as if lost to Him, when we become losers.

A Request

Once I was preaching and became very thirsty. I even mentioned my thirst from the pulpit. Afterward a friend told me that the Holy Spirit had asked him to fetch me a glass of water, but he was too self-conscious to do so. He was very grieved with himself and apologetic. It was such a simple and logical request that it seemed to be beyond him.

Globally Minded

We say that it's good and we're glad that the problems of this world are ultimately God's to solve and not ours. But it is healthy at times to think about the state that the world would be in if it truly were all up to us. And I mean to include in that the condition of things locally among our own friends, family, and acquaintances. I sense that the time is now at hand that God is beginning to raise the awareness of His people into a more global awareness and to extend our consciousness further to include a sensitivity to more of our neighbors. He must do this to overcome our self-centeredness and preoccupation with our own church and family circles in order to prepare us to rule and reign with Christ during the Millennium when we will *have* to be more globally minded and others-oriented. People will be looking to us then as an extension of His ruling arm, as they are beginning even now to do. So there is a balance to be struck between allowing ourselves to be crushed by the weight of the world's burdens and a seemingly scot-free irresponsibility of a total ignorance of those burdens; one extreme is as misguided as the other. We could begin with a question of ourselves like: If I were God, what do I think would demand my most urgent attention now as I look upon my world? And then pray and act accordingly. It would behoove some of us, who pride ourselves on being worry-free, to "worry" a little more about others.

Orphans

Why should we reflect the Father's heart in reaching out to orphans and widows, and to foreigners? Because before He touched us, we were orphans without a heavenly Father, and we were without a heavenly Husband, and estranged from the Body of Christ, we were not a people.

The Cross

We are learning to live at the cross. We are learning that all must be brought through the cross, all that concerns a disciple of Jesus Christ. To live at the cross means that all that you are and have and want is passing through the cross. For something of ours to pass through the cross means that we taste and experience what it is like not to be or have while still being or having. That is, we exist or possess in a different dimension now, a dimension of consciousness that things could be a different or opposite way. It is a new way of holding people and things and times gently as if almost not to hold them. It is God's way.

"But this I say, brethren, the time is short: it remains, that both they that have wives be as though they had none; and they that weep, as though they wept not; and they that rejoice, as though they rejoiced not; and they that buy, as though they possessed not; and they that use this world, as not abusing it: for the fashion of this world passes away" (1 Cor. 7, v. 29–31).

Climbing

There is no experience, no spiritual level to be reached in God that will not eventually grow stale if there is no intention of going further. God designed it that way to keep us hungry for Him. He knows we cannot stay long on any plateau. Unless we press forward, we will automatically fall backward, and that is allowed by Him. Those who continue to press and to knock are those who grow nearest to Him. Like Peter and Andrew or James and John of the Master's inner circle, it takes pairs of brothers or sisters to help each other climb.

Overflowing

Jesus said, "Father, if it be possible, let this cup pass from me." It was the cup that was overflowing with appointed sufferings. It still overflows into our lives as believers. And because His sufferings overflow, so do the consolations and the comfort through His Holy Spirit, our Comforter.

Guilt

No sooner does the gospel create guilt within us than it removes that same guilt forever, but nevertheless it must first create it. The bad news has to precede the good news. After all, it was our sin that separated Jesus from His Father for the first and only time, which is what actually killed him.

Deliverance

When Moses first approached Pharaoh with God's command to set His people free, not only did he get no positive results but Pharaoh decided to worsen the peoples' condition by insisting that they gather their own straw for bricks. When deliverance begins in any area in our lives, things often seem to get worse instead of better to see if we will become discouraged and doubt God's promise to us.

Power

When Moses was appointed to lead the people of Israel out of Egypt, he expostulated with God that the people would not believe his message. It was then that God began to show him the power that he would demonstrate in the presence of Pharaoh. Similarly Jesus, after he had commissioned the apostles, spoke of the powerful signs that would follow their preaching, as if to honor and validate it in the presence of all who would see and hear. Casting out devils, healing the sick, and even taking up serpents, which is what Moses did at God's command, and the serpent became his rod again. That shepherd's rod would be so instrumental in the coming displays of power, as that shepherding instinct will be so instrumental in us today.

Opposites

These four things are the opposite of what we might expect them to be: natural fire burns hotter the closer we approach while God's all-consuming fire burns hotter the farther we run from it. Natural children learn independence from their parents while our Heavenly Father teaches us to be dependent. Surrender in a natural war means we've lost, while surrender in the spirit brings certain victory. Pouring out the contents of a cup leaves it empty, but pouring out our contents as spiritual vessels leaves us brimming full.

Addendum

Raised

Until we understand how profoundly we were affected by our own upbringing or the lack of it, we will not have power to comprehend how much more profoundly we have been impacted and continue to be impacted by our rebirth to a spiritual parent. First comes the natural and then the spiritual. First comes the understanding of how deeply we've been marked by our upbringing, and continue to be, so as to better appreciate the power and depth of the divine intervention that changes our nature.

Imprinting

The first face that Adam ever beheld was the face of God. This took place in the instant of his maximum impressionability, the most formative moment in his life, as he gazed upon the One in whose image he had just been made.

We too, in our peak microseconds of malleability, when we entered the Last Adam, beheld the face of God in the Spirit and had His image burned within us in the most profound depths of our being, where we will never forget it and from whence we will each draw increasingly and instinctively our own unique identities which are being conformed irresistibly to that Image.

Becoming

I become who I am, and I am who I become.

Becoming is linked to being. So that when we appear to be doing nothing, we are actually moving ahead. The surrounding culture will only grudgingly allow this kind of progress as it does not regard it as progress but instead as loss and waste. The surrounding culture has mistakenly linked *doing* to becoming.

We become what we are in Christ already: holy.

At the same time, we become what we are not yet. We become what we have not been, thus moving beyond ourselves, occupying new territory of identity.

When we, as His bride, become irresistible to Him, He will return for us.

Obedience

Whatever is not done in obedience to God is lawlessness. "Whatever is not of faith is sin." Whatever is not done in obedience to God is lawlessness, no matter how "good" the deed or well-intentioned.

Our obedience to Him brings intimacy in relation to Him, just as our submission to one another tends to bring greater intimacy with one another.

Jesus is in such intimate union with His Father because of His utter submission to the will of His Father.

We are to give ourselves to God to the furthest extent that it is given us to conceive of being given to God . . . no margin of conscious withholding.

Should Do

For a believer, pride is a sin, and one's service to God is regarded as a privilege rather than an obligation. Within the sphere of that service, one should not impose many "shoulds" because that is to impose condemnation, which is a hindrance to growth.

A well-meaning parent, who had been exposed to teaching of the above-mentioned truth, approached another parent at a college graduation to say, "You should be—no, I mean you have to be—no, I mean you get to be proud of—no, I mean you must be happy with your daughter—that is, you must be tickled with her achievements."

Relationships

We have heard it said that Christianity is a relationship, not a religion. It is a relationship with Jesus Christ, first and foremost, and from that, we draw our acceptance and security to venture into other relationships. At which points that we enter into other relationships, there Christianity becomes a relationship with a neighbor or a family member, or a spouse, or an employer or whatever the case may be. Christianity, or the lack of it, is evidenced in all our relationships, because Christianity is relationship in a life full of relationships, including, as a friend reminded me, my relationship with myself! (I offer this characterization for the relationships of a dysfunctional family: half are jokers and the other half can't take a joke! At Thanksgiving, they are a bunch of turkeys living a lifestyle of stuffing and denial.)

Sifting Winds

The soldiers blindfolded Jesus and then beat him, demanding that he "prophesy" who had struck him. He couldn't see the blows coming and so he couldn't brace himself. The soldiers did that for a reason; they wanted him more vulnerable and they wanted him to feel more pain.

Harry Houdini died of a ruptured appendix in 1926 because a jokester hit him in the stomach when he wasn't expecting it. It was a college student who had heard Houdini's boast that no one could hurt him. He had not had time to brace himself. He died on Halloween.

Now is the time for God's people to brace themselves for what may be coming soon. We will not be devastated by the coming storm if we take time to tense our spiritual muscles and prepare.

Jesus will not separate the sheep from the goats by mere words. He will allow tribulation to do the sifting and separating. The true character and identity of each rises speedily to the surface in the time of trial.

Love

To be falling in love with Jesus means to be falling in love with people, more and more people, so many people as to make it an exercise in futility to try to pursue any single one of them. In full, the closer we get to Jesus, the more everyone looks familiar.

Creative

Praise creates new pathways and unstops old pathways for blessings to flow into our lives and the lives of those we love.

But Lucifer, that erstwhile master of the praise became more concerned with the blessings than with the relationship of praise and adoration. He thought he could use God for His many benefits. And in pursuit of that end, he became the prototype for the contemporary woman who desires and proposes a child by a man with whom she has no desire for a relationship, and thus no intention of allowing that man to be a husband to her or a father to the child. At that point, the point where he put the proverbial cart before the horse, Satan ceased being truly creative and began to be merely crafty.

It's Show Time

It is not enough to experience victory; we must triumph. You say, "If I could just taste more victory, I would be happy; forget the triumph." Though triumph is the celebration of victory, paradoxically, until we partake of triumph, we cannot gain more victory. Maybe we haven't properly celebrated the victories already gained, and, then too, we need to remember the people of Israel, who went into battle celebrating victory before a hand had been raised to fight. In the triumphal processions of the Roman generals, the captives trailed along behind in chains, as trophies of the conquest. Some were allowed to scream insults at the generals, to keep them humble.

So too in our triumphal celebration, the demonic spirits must fall in line behind us as trophies of Christ's conquest over them at the cross. "And having spoiled principalities and powers, he made a show of them openly, triumphing over them in it" (Colossians 2, v. 15).

You might say it was "show time" for Jesus and His church. Our triumphant praise reminds the demons that they are bound in helpless procession to their inevitable doom!

Counsel Despite Myself

One of the ways we can know the spirit of counsel is moving within us is when we hear ourselves saying something so contrary to our own self-interest and natural inclination that our self cries out within us where only we can hear, "Why are you saying that, that won't achieve the desired goal; you're going in the opposite direction!"

Then, too, the time will eventually come when we must summon the boldness to say what seems on the surface a selfish and even manipulative opinion but really isn't because we have patiently waited for the appropriate time to express it from a motive that was being purified during the waiting period.

Perhaps even Jesus's anger was refined as He sat plaiting the cords of the whip He would use to drive out the moneychangers.

Amplification and Application

Another reason for us to keep our hearts with all diligence is that the intentions and thoughts of the heart are amplified into the ear of God over a kind of inner megaphone or intercom such that we might as well be shouting into heaven.

When we "chew on" the words of God, our spirits secrete a kind of "saliva," known as faith, which aids in "digestion" (application) (Hebrews 4:1–2).